nine ladies dan

...-leaping

...ers piping

7.95

TOYS AND MODELS

A Sourcebook of Ideas by
Rodney Peppé

Clockwork Bus (see page 106)

TOYS AND MODELS

A Sourcebook of Ideas by
Rodney Peppé

ANTIQUE COLLECTORS' CLUB

For Georgia and Blair

British Library Cataloguing-in-Publication Data
A catalogue record for this book is available from the British Library

Printed in England
Published by the Antique Collectors' Club Ltd., Woodbridge, Suffolk

CONTENTS

By a model denotes that a plan is available for this toy

For eighteen months my exhibition 'Toy with the Idea' toured England and Wales under the auspices of the Area Museums Council for the South West. The first venue was the Corinium Museum, Cirencester, in May 1994. Here, the children are being shown my favourite toy, 'Luigi', a slightly portly, over-the-hill acrobat who performs for two minutes with the aid of a sand motor.
Gloucestershire County Museums

'The Mice Who Lived in a Shoe' is based upon two models I made to draw the pictures: a skeleton framework and the complete shoe-house itself. Here, I am explaining to the young audience at the Corinium Museum my method of drawing from my models and inserting the mice family (all ten of them) into the pictures.
Gloucestershire County Museums

INTRODUCTION

Some twenty years ago I was asked to write a book on toymaking. The result was *Rodney Peppé's Moving Toys,* now out of print. The book dealt, mainly, with simple mechanisms from the past redesigned for the present, with plans for making every toy.

In this book, *Toys and Models: A Sourcebook of Ideas,* I want to go further, exploring the nature of toys and getting ideas for making them. It is essentially a sourcebook of toy ideas, which draws from my own work as a children's author-artist using toys and models as reference for picturebooks. The book is for anyone who would like to make toys, models or automata, or would do so, if only they had the time!

I deal in the currency of ideas, which fuel any project. The stronger they are the more potent the project becomes. In the IDEA and TOY WITH THE IDEA sections the process of getting ideas is closely examined. Particular attention is paid to the building of an idea to support subsidiary ideas.

As a sourcebook, by definition, the illustrations should provide the reader with a stimulus to the imagination. They should be used as such, like a springboard to launch one's own personal flight; not to slavishly copy. To see one thing and express another is ultimately more rewarding.

Ready examples for fostering original work by these means are provided by schools and children's libraries. They decorate their walls with children's work which is often based on the picture books they read. The children's creative antennae are further alerted by visiting authors and illustrators who boost their imaginations in all sorts of ways.

If this works for children, why not for adults? It can, but whereas children, and especially very young children, have a special energy for creativity, adults are more inhibited; unless they work in a creative environment. One only has to see how small children express themselves with complete abandon in their artwork, to acknowledge the truth of this.

Where the adult scores, however, is in manual dexterity. It is comforting to know that your average four year-old genius could not attempt any of the toys and models in these pages! As they grow older some children do become clever with their hands and what they lose in their early artistry they gain in skills such as modelmaking. I've seen shoe-houses, kettleships and flying baskets which, though based on my models, are clearly original works by children. They have taken the leap by absorbing, not copying the reference.

If, in producing their own versions of my work, I have engaged children's imaginations, giving a mere nudge in which direction to go, I can certainly do the same for adults. Anyone, in fact, who would like to take the leap.

The springboard is ready.

TOY

What is a toy? Any dictionary will tell us: *A plaything esp. for a child.* A string of definitions follow, but we still have to search our own minds for a satisfying explanation.

In the film *Citizen Kane,* Orson Welles as Kane breathes out one word, 'Rosebud'. It is his last. At the end of the film, after a series of flashbacks, we discover that Rosebud was the name painted on his favourite toy, a sledge. We watch it and the junk of a lifetime burning in the incinerator. As the painted letters writhe and peel away in the flames we, the audience, see that from all his treasures it is Rosebud, a mere toy, which claims Kane's last breath.

That is a toy.

Most of us have lost our childhood toys, perhaps not as dramatically as Kane, but destruction or disintegration is a common fate for many a plaything. True, some are played to death, which gives them even more character than they ever had; and they survive in that state well into the adult lives of their owners. But why are toys so important to a child?

Just as children belong to their parents, so they need something to belong to them. Perhaps this is why they find their toys and pets such significant parts of their lives. For they are, after all, their friends, featuring in their childhood games. But do toys have a purpose beyond being companions for a child's imagination? Perhaps, in some way they prepare them for adult life. Certainly, their emotions are involved and by no means in a surrogate way. The reality of a child's relationship to a toy is just as potent as any forged in real-life.

Many toys are miniatures of life-sized creatures and objects. They enable children to participate on their own level, in real-life situations. The games and stories they devise around their toys lead, eventually, to creative endeavour and self expression. The process, in fact, is not unlike making art.

There clearly is a relationship between toys and art. One only has to look at Picasso's playful sculptures, juxtaposing toy elements, or his frolicsome ceramics, to see the connection. We can also trace the giant mobiles by Alexander Calder to his genesis as a toymaker, especially when we remember the renowned *Calder's Circus.* This was contained in five suitcases and Calder himself acted as ringmaster and operator of his articulated circus troupe. Everything was made from corks and wire and bits of string.

Are these examples by modern masters art or toys? Art, certainly, but it is doubtful that we could call them toys. Surely, one should be able to play with a toy, an activity denied by the very nature of a work of art. And if playing participation is the sole criterion, how stands the cardboard box or a paper bag? These objects can engage a child's imagination as much as any toy!

I recall an incident when I was eight years old. A household mop was standing outside my aunt's kitchen window. I struck up a conversation with the mop, holding it by the handle, animating it like a puppet. The mop responded by shaking or nodding its head to my enquiries. Suddenly I caught sight of my aunt smiling, watching me through the window. I blushed and returned the mop to its inanimate state and original position. The spell was broken and the balloon of invention burst.

What had been, for a brief creative moment, an imaginative albeit surrogate, responsive toy became once more a mere household object. So mops are not toys, neither are cardboard boxes or paper bags! A toy should always be a toy. There doesn't seem to be any one particular word to describe a toy, but if we scan the following list, we may make some connections:

AMUSEMENT, ATTRACTIVENESS, COMFORT, DISCOVERY, DIVERSION, EMOTION, ESCAPISM, FLEXIBILITY (of interpretation), FUN, IMAGINATION, INGENUITY, INSTRUCTION, INVENTION, PARTICIPATION, PLEASURE, SELF-REALIZATION, STIMULATION, TACTILITY, UNIVERSALITY (of appeal), WONDER.

If we then try to think of what is the ideal toy, it is surely the one that pleases us the most. We all have our own Rosebud.

TOY

BALANCING TOYS

STRING TOYS

HAND-OPERATED MODELS AND AUTOMATA

SLOT-TOGETHER TOYS

Balancing Tumblers

The ancestor of this toy was made from metal rods and featured solid, three-dimensional clowns. I have redesigned it for the scroll saw as a very simple but effective toy to make. The running time is forty seconds; that is the time it takes the tumblers to reach the bottom of the frame. It's a very pretty action to watch, as they rotate gently forwards and then backwards to their destination.

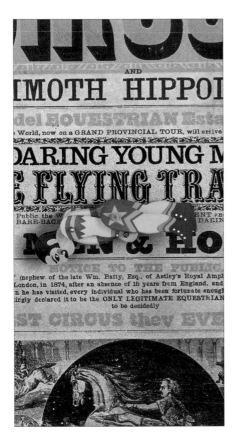

Sand-Toy 'Leotard'

This is my favourite toy and one that intrigued little Victorians. The fascination lies in the near magical machinery that works the acrobat. In the back of the box there is some silver sand in the base. When the box is turned over slowly to the right the sand gathers on to a V-shaped shelf at the top of the box and then trickles through a hole on to a small replica of a watermill wheel. This is attached to a spindle and activates 'Leotard'. (J. Leotard invented the flying trapeze in 1859.) Being jointed at the limbs and neck enables him to perform innumerable and intricate movements in an unpredictable sequence.

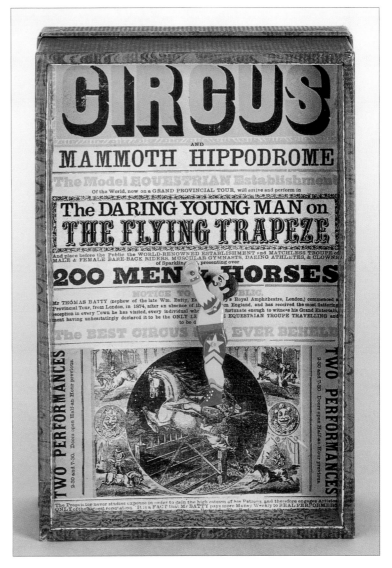

Rocking Horse
This piece is based on a 19th century watercolour, using modern trimmings to decorate the horse. The horse itself is made in three sections as shown below. The stirrups are soldering wire, pinched at the base with pliers. The saddle is soft suede and the girth coloured felt. The brasses are punched from metallic card.

Tivoli Acrobats
...so called, because they are based on a Victorian game of that name. Their appeal, especially to very young children, lies in the ability of the acrobats to act as a team. Feed a ball into the top clown's cup and its weight transfers the ball into the next cup. While the first clown counterbalances backwards, the second passes the ball to the third who repeats the operation; and the fourth clown drops the ball on to the bell which gives out a satisfying 'ting'. The ball then rolls on to the board and one scores as in a game of Bagatelle.

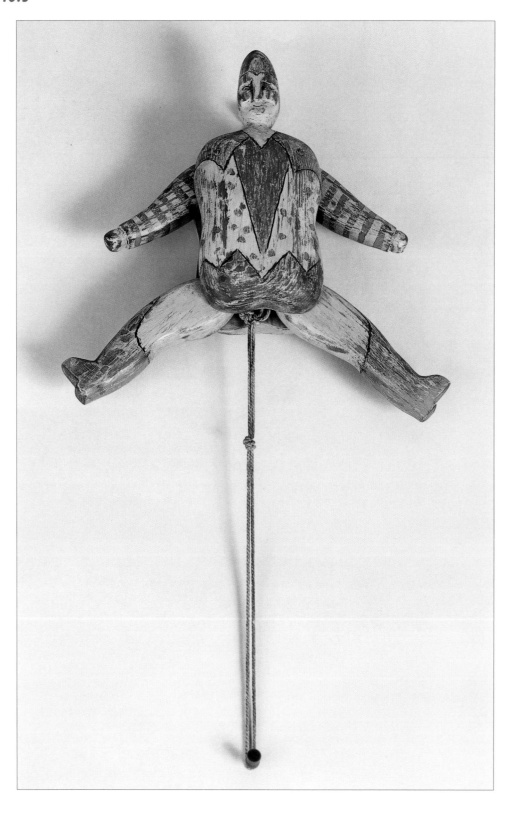

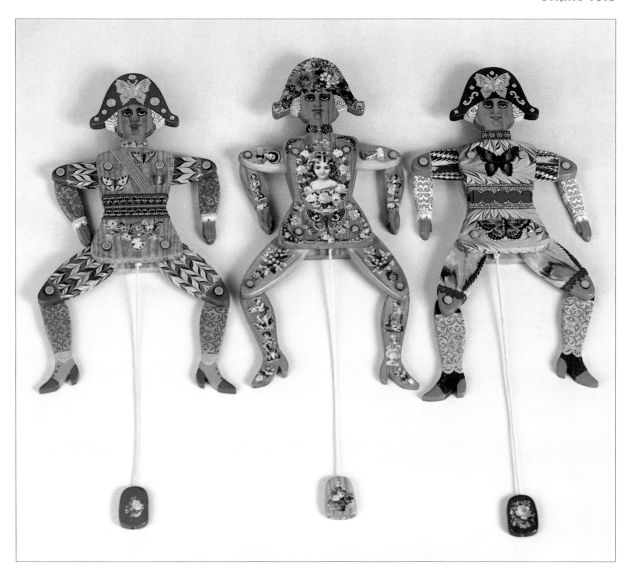

Jumping Jack or Pantin (above)

The mechanics of this simple toy were known to the Egyptians, but its real popularity was marked by a childish craze which swept Paris in 1746. Soon, adults were playing with the *Pantin*, named after its place of origin.

Its popularity lasted for a decade when it was eventually banned by the police, who reasoned that women, under the lively influence of this continual jumping, were in danger of bearing babies with twisted limbs!

'Old' Jumping Jack (opposite)

This is my 'homage' to an old American jumping jack, circa 1800. I enjoy making fakes!

Circus Lion Pull-Toy
This lion wags his tail, shakes his head and rolls his eyes when pulled or pushed along. He is based on an illustration from one of my own picture books, but the mechanism, like the Drummer's, page 27, is taken from Edlin dolls of the early 19th century. You may know it better as the crankshaft.

Climbing Monkey
This is an adaptation of a 1903 tin toy. The action fascinates because the monkey really does climb the string. The secret is in the double drum mechanism which enables the monkey to move up the string when it is pulled, and down when it is relaxed.

Blinking Owl
This is my homage to the 19th century innovator of toy books, Lothar Meggendorfer. The blink mechanism is adapted from one of his movable books worked by card levers. But the Owl is based on one of my own children's book illustrations.

The mechanics of the blink are remarkably life-like. On pulling out the tab the Owl doesn't merely shut his eyes and then open them on the return of the tab. He blinks: open-shut-open, in one pull, or push of the lever. He flaps his wings and tail at the same time, for good measure.

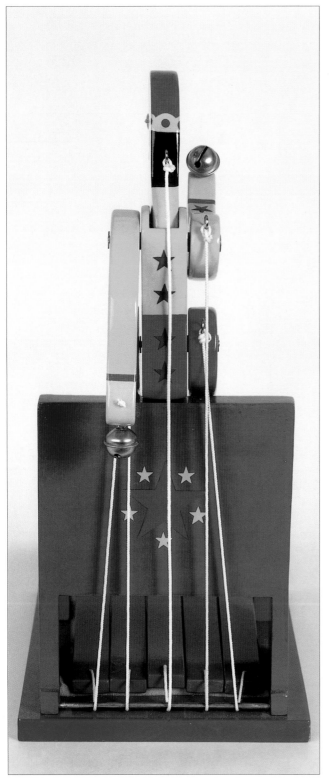

Musical Clown Bell-Toy

This toy is based on an illustration from Victor Bonnet's 1925 catalogue of Martin toys, showing 'Le Clown Orchestre'.

The mechanics were not shown in the picture, so I had to invent my own. Each finger-pedal attached by a string moves a part of the clown's body, to the accompaniment of small bells. The larger version was made as a 'hands on' piece for exhibition.

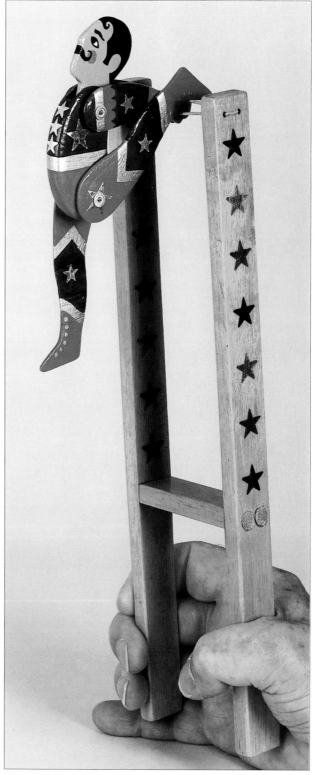

Torsion Toy Acrobat

Most children have had a torsion toy at some time, and its popularity through the ages is doubtless based upon the feeling of complete control one has over the actions. The pressure applied to the base of the sticks stretches the twisted string so as to make the acrobat somersault at will and even stop in mid air.

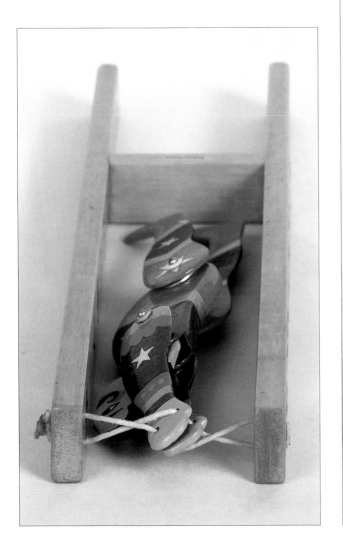

Hand Cranked Drummer

In the 1820s, toys with very simple hand-wound movements were being sold in London. One shop which sold such toys was called Edlin's Rational Repository of Amusement and Instruction! The mechanism of the Edlin dolls is used for this toy. A wooden crank handle turns a roller concealed in the platform base. This winds two separate strings simultaneously, but in alternating rhythm.

I made a large version of this toy, commissioned by the Friends of Cheltenham Art Gallery and Museums to serve as a Donations Box. A photo-electric cell, activated by insertion of notes or coins, enabled the drummer to 'drum up support'.

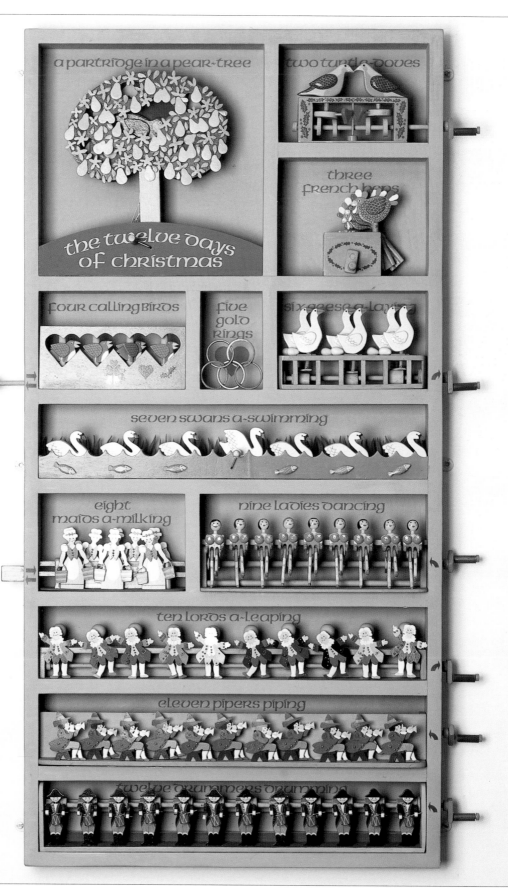

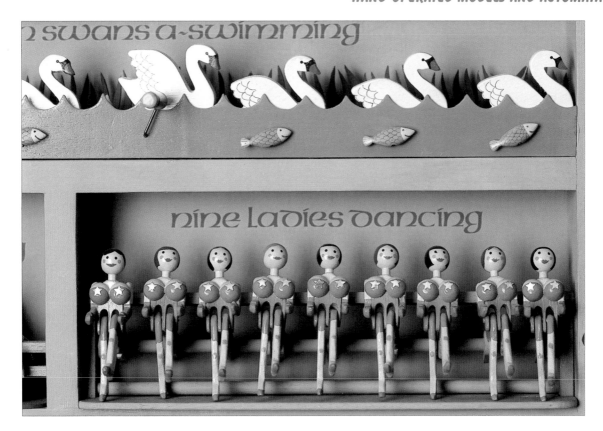

The Twelve Days of Christmas

I made this piece during 1990, between bouts of scriptwriting the *Huxley Pig* TV series. My purpose was to discover and invent simple mechanisms – each one different. Here are brief descriptions of the actions:

> *The Partridge* appears and disappears in the foliage.
> *Two Turtle Doves* turn to and from each other, with a brief kiss – or is it a nod?
> *Three French Hens* peck at corn, in rotation.
> *Four Calling Birds* swivel in and out of their heart-shaped windows.
> *Five Gold Rings* aren't gold and don't move.
> *Six Geese a-Laying* hop up and down in pairs.
> *Seven Swans a-Swimming* bob among the waves followed by the fish.
> *Eight Maids a-Milking* sway from side to side.
> *Nine Ladies Dancing* kick their legs in unison. They are 'The Bluebelles'.
> *Ten Lords a-Leaping* jump and sway in celebratory mood.
> *Eleven Pipers Piping* tap their feet and nod their heads.
> *Twelve Drummers Drumming* strike four beats to the bar.

Directional arrows show whether to turn the handles clockwise or anti-clockwise. One eager collector silenced my trumpeters with a wrong turn. Luckily I had designed the sections to be removed for repair. It's important to leave 'escape hatches' when making automata.

Bicarus (above)

Originally designed to be electrically operated with an 8rpm motor, the torque was insufficient to drive Bicarus over long periods in exhibitions. Like his near namesake Icarus, who flew too near to the sun, he showed signs of distress, doing embarrassing 'wheelies'.

I altered Bicarus to hand cranked operation and entrusted him to the care of my younger son Jonathan, a painter and sculptor.

Peace on Earth (Lion and Lamb) (opposite)

Pull the Lion's tail and peace is but a memory! A simple counterweight provides the action. As the Lion's paw springs up, his jaw drops to reveal fearsome teeth and red eyes. The Lamb, in terror, jerks up his head. My marbling experiments are evident. I have made several versions using marbled paper or painted backgrounds.

Uncle Sam's Whirligig I

Whirligigs first appeared in the mountainous wood-carving regions of medieval Europe. They became popular in America in the early 19th century where their appeal still survives.

On a visit to New England I was fascinated by these modern folk-art pieces, often quite crudely carved. My little model is, for me, a memento of my visit, neatly side-stepping the carving issue by being cut out with a scroll saw. It also breaks the rules by being hand-cranked.

Uncle Sam's Whirligig II
With my second, much later, version of this whirligig I tried to emulate a folk-art look. Made from driftwood collected on Norfolk beaches it still retains a tang of the sea.

As it didn't respond too well to the wind, I added the crank handle. Both mechanically and artistically it's a fake. But then I love making fakes. I've resisted rubbing off the paint and engraining it with dust!

Double Headed Strongman

The dumb-bell head is a notion lifted from the surrealist painter, Magritte. Whereas his heads were blank mine show, alternately at the turn of a wrist, a macho mustachioed face and a softer, more poetic face, shedding a tear. I have made several of the larger scale models and toyed with the idea of making electrically-operated ones.

Scissors Toy Soldiers

The idea of the scissors toy goes back to the 16th century. They are sometimes called 'lazy tongs' after those used by confectioners. Very popular in Saxony, they often took the form of soldiers. My troop have completely fabricated uniforms and could belong to any army.

It's a simple but repetitive toy to make. The effect, though, is very decorative and well worth the effort. You could have ten soldiers if you have the patience to recruit them! I settled for seven.

Tyger! Tyger!
William Blake's famous poem was the inspiration for this, one of my larger pieces. The hand cranked wired movements from two handles control the tiger's walk, head mechanism and the birds 'flying' on wires in the marbled MDF jungle.

tyger! tyger! burning bright
in the forests of the night;
what immortal hand or eye
could frame thy fearful symmetry?

From The Tyger by William Blake (1757-1832)

Hollywood Sign

The disparate letters in the famous HOLLYWOOD sign cry out for animation. Why, even static, they look as if they are moving! Driving around Los Angeles they suddenly appear from nowhere, insistently reminding you of where you are.

It is my favourite graphic icon, not only because it represents the beloved Dream Factory, where my elder son is an editor, but because its visual impact is astonishing.

Mechanically, the piece is very simple. The letters ride up and down on pegs activated by a series of cams fixed at various angles on a bar. The star moves by friction on a rotating base resting on a moving disc at the end of the bar.

Hooray for Hollywood!
Another version, with a slightly different noisier mechanism, uses short battens, as cams, to lift longer battens upon which the letters ride. A wave effect is set up while the star rotates. I made this for my film editor son, with his picture in the star. But he modestly kept it facing inwards.

The Thin Blue Line

A Victorian photograph is both the inspiration and *raison d'être* for this automaton. Mechanically, it works on the same principle as the 'Hollywood Sign' (page 38). As the Union Jack twirls around on a friction driven pole, the British 'Bobbies' (named after Sir Robert Peel who established the London police force) 'bob' up and down.

Ark Toy

The mechanism employed here is the Geneva Wheel which works on the same principle as a film projector, stepping the film on one frame at a time. As the handle is turned, animals appear on deck, colour matching their mates. The dove on the rain-cloud moves up and down separately from the elephant since they are on different cams.

The Blinking Imp

A cigar box and a glass negative of my enlarged thumbprint provide the means to create this piece. To operate the blink mechanism a camera cable release pushes up and releases a pink card to effect the blink. I debated whether to add a halo to the performance but decided to adopt the KISS principle (Keep It Simple Stupid). I now wonder if I missed a trick.

*Hole-and-Peg Acrobats

The figures are designed so that they can slot into each other with little pegs. The pegs are interchangeable with hands and feet so that many positional permutations can be achieved. It makes an interesting rearrangeable shelf-piece.

Bird Trees
These are based on a Japanese idea. They play dual roles of decorative shelf-pieces and puzzles.

Birds and Worm Puzzle
A little puzzle for a little person. But take care the pieces aren't swallowed!

*Money Box
Six modules cut from skin-ply, painted or decorated with collage, make up this simple-to-assemble money box. A different design applied to the interior gives you double your money!

Punch and Judy Show
Probably the most popular folk play in the English language, 'Punch and Judy' is now desperately politically incorrect! I considered excluding it from this book, not wishing to offend. However taking a longer view with some regard for tradition, I included it – with apologies to adherents of p.c.

Goldilocks and the Three Bears
The well-known fairy tale comes to life as you build up the pieces into Father Bear, Mother Bear, Baby Bear and Goldilocks. There's also a bed, a chair and a porridge plate and spoon as additional props.

Decorative Alphabet
Based on the typeface 'Sinaloa' this alphabet can be used for anything but teaching the alphabet! The letters are far too sophisticated but ideal for decorative application.

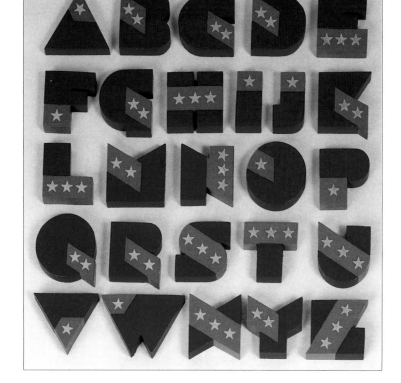

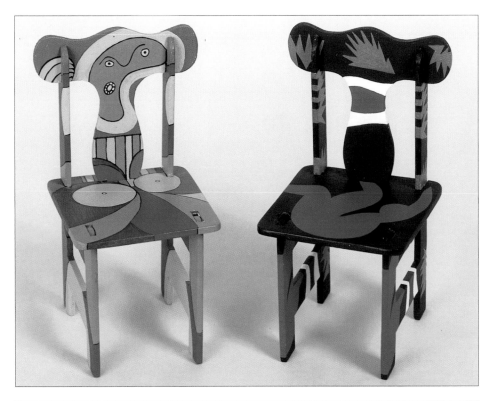

Artists' Chairs
My homage to four of the 20th century's greatest artists: Picasso, Matisse, Miró and Klee.

Alphabet Chair
A larger version of the slot-together chair, decorated with stencilled letters.

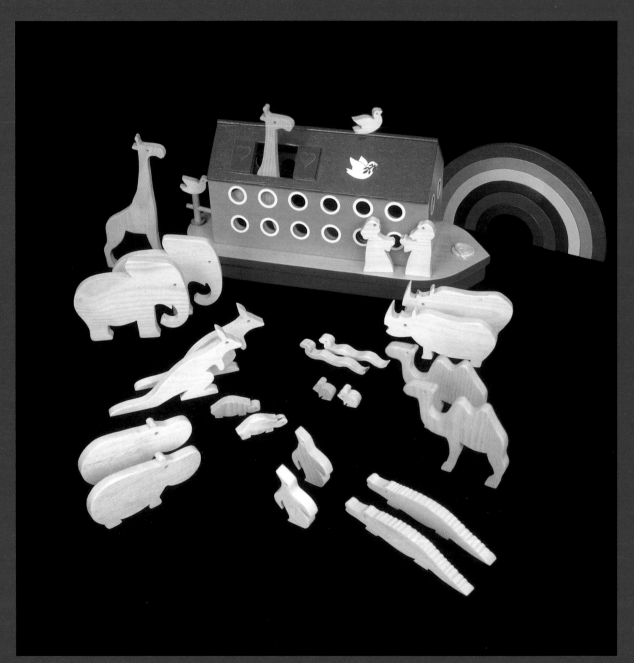

Photograph: Vincent Oliver

IDEA

The crucial moment for any project is the instant when we get the idea for it. It's not easy to capture that moment. Sometimes it's a flash of sudden insight. At other times it's a slow, plodding process of pushing and pulling the notions into shape. Whichever route the idea chooses, its arrival is acknowledged by our imagination. A 'click' occurs and we say 'That's it!' And it usually is.

It isn't always that easy, and seldom is in any creative endeavour. Bearing this in mind let us follow a course of discovery by confronting a creative problem: to invent a simple automaton. Its legend is PEACE ON EARTH.

Suppose we start with the proverbial blank sheet of white paper believed to be an abundant breeding ground for ideas. Our pencils are poised, awaiting the muse to strike. Nothing happens. The paper seems, if anything, to become even whiter.

If we ignore it, that's not a defeat; merely a retreat. The mind is being given a chance to slip into neutral and relax. A break would do us good, and we forget the problem. We go for a drive, meet a friend, or have a drink. Just as we are negotiating a bend in the road, or talking to a friend, the problem is solved. A 'click' occurs and we say 'That's it!' While we had forgotten about the problem, the problem had not forgotten us.

That's a nice and easy way to get an idea, but suppose we are not so lucky. The very white and very blank sheet of white paper is still before us. We must make a mark, written, doodled or scribbled. Anything to remove that whiteness! Some of the marks may look interesting, perhaps even intriguing enough to start a train of thought. The mind is in gear to move forward... but our train hits the buffers! Pity. It was looking good, and then suddenly it wasn't.

It often happens that way – the elements, the marks and doodles, don't amount to anything, try as we might to connect them. Trial and error is our only chance, since chance itself has bypassed us.

We crunch up the piece of paper, but instead of throwing it away, say we examine it, slowly turning it round. It's like a multi-faceted abstract sculpture. As the light plays on its contours, images flood the mind. One may be the head of a LION. Now we are getting somewhere: we need something to play against the LION – an unlikely partner preferably, because unlikely partners make the best elements for ideas.

How else can we alter the piece of paper? We can straighten it out and notice that the crumpled surface, in a strong light, looks like a choppy SEA. We make the connection: SEA LION – But there is no idea there, not for PEACE ON EARTH.

Our flattened, crumpled piece of paper looks exhausted. But it isn't. We can distress it further: wet it, burn it, tear it up. We tear it up, push the pieces around and study them. Nothing happens, and in desperation we screw up the pieces. And then it happens! They look like a flock of white sheep.

SHEEP! Of course. And at last we make the connection, with a little adjustment: THE LION AND THE LAMB, symbols for PEACE ON EARTH. The tortuous empirical path led us, eventually, to the solution which enables us to make the automaton set in the problem. Pull the Lion's tail and see him roar as the Lamb reacts in cheeky mock terror! (page 30).

Our individual approaches and methods for getting ideas are as different and personal as our handwriting. But there are general guidelines we can follow. Conversely, the more crooked the path we choose the better are our chances of finding the unexpected.

We should really train our minds to behave like wayward supermarket trolleys, which take you in every direction, except in the one you want to go! That way lies the unexpected and we arrive, as if by chance, at the solution we seek. A 'straight' trolley will merely take you where everybody else is going… to cliché-land where the spurious bargain offers beckon! We must use serendipity and look for the accident to suggest the idea.

Hidden connections, unlikely partners, anomalies – these are all grist to the mill. We see something but look at it in a different way. Twist it and turn it like our screwed up piece of paper which heralded the LION and the LAMB by mere mental play. Sometimes the most extraordinary mental acrobatics, requiring leaps in the imagination, yield, like the crooked trolley, the most unexpected and satisfying results.

Much of what we produce will end up in the dustbin, but that is one of the most useful tools we possess. We must be the editors of our own creations, being mindful that the best ideas are the simplest. The ones, when we say to ourselves, 'why didn't I think of that before?' Chances are, nobody else did either!

IDEA

MOTORIZED PICTURES

ELECTRIC MODELS AND AUTOMATA

AUTOMATED CLOCKS

HOUSE BOXES

Wobbly Cone Illusion (left)
An 8rpm motor works this fascinating, hypnotic, two-dimensional design. As it rotates, it appears to wobble as a three-dimensional cone.

Marcel Duchamp created optical discs, *roto-reliefs* for his 1926 film, *Anémic Cinema*. Later he created coloured discs which, as they rotated, appeared to expand and contract, creating an illusion of depth.

Solar Toy Acrobat (below left)
A small motor powers a solar panel which turns the Harlequin on a spindle. The stronger the light source the faster he goes. His speed is governed by the brightness of sunlight or an electric bulb.

(Opposite)
Jungle from Rodney Peppé's PUZZLE BOOK
A longcase clock movement, with a striking train, provided me with an ideal mechanism to animate my jungle picture. Pulleys and flexible steel drive-bands govern the performance of each creature. Here's what they do:

Lion: shakes his head from side to side. *Sun:* rotates clockwise. *Monkey:* shakes his fist and chatters. *Toucan:* opens and closes his beak and flaps his wings. *Leopard:* waves her paw. *Elephant:* nods his head. *Rhino:* just misses spiking the Elephant. *Frog:* jumps up and down. *Owl:* Blinks and flaps her wings. *Snake:* nods his head. *Hippo:* shakes his head. *Tortoise:* pokes his head in and out of his shell. *Parrot:* nods his head. *Butterfly:* twitches. *Giraffe:* munches leaves. *Caterpillar:* wriggles. *Tiger:* shakes her head. *Hunter:* bobs back and forth hiding behind leaves. *Crocodile:* snaps his jaws and swishes his tail.

Boat with 3 Fish
An 8rpm motor, turning a disc anti-clockwise turns an adjacent disc clockwise.
This starts up three sets of waves, arranged in depth and moves the boat up
and down.

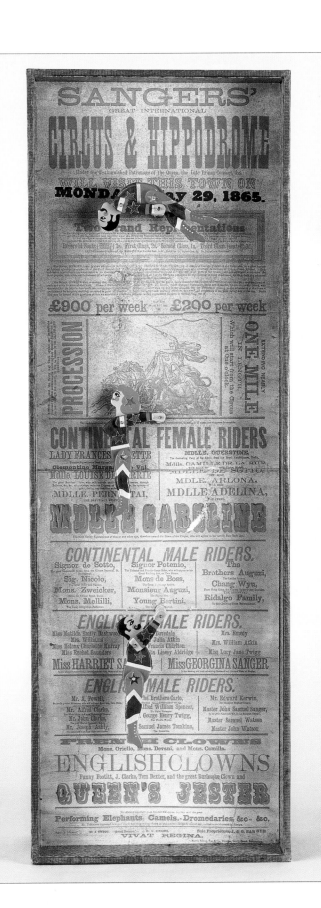

3 Trapeze Artistes
Originally a clockwork piece, I connected this model to an electric 8rpm motor for exhibitions. The direction of the acrobats can be governed by twisting over the drive band on its pulley at the back.

Uncle Sam Cyclist
A short piece of thin dowel acts as a cam to push the torso forward as Uncle Sam circumvents the track. He has worn a groove in it – a testament to his indefatigable cycling over a period of 18 months in a touring exhibition.

Cyclist, Training his Dog in the Park

As with the *Uncle Sam cyclist*, opposite, and the *Bicycle Clock* on page 71, a small dowel cam serves to project the torso forward at each contact. That little extra thrust to the cycling action enhances the performance immeasurably. It is driven by a 6rpm motor.

But let's not forget the dog's performance. As dogs do, the dog does. On each circuit at a certain point she squats, then slowly rises, continuing her walk on the lengthy leash.

Serendipity played its part here. The dog's performance is governed by the pressure of the bar holding her to the ground. As the base is not absolutely level the discrepancy allows for the call of nature to be addressed.

A Different Drummer

This is, perhaps, my most personal piece. As I mention at the end of the *Toy with the Idea* section, page 96, the sentiment conveyed by Thoreau's words expresses perfectly my role as a toy and model maker and indeed automatist.

The action of the drummer is governed by rotating cams and friction discs. A bevel gear turns the flag powered by an 8rpm motor, which also drives a fishing reel mechanism. It is this that allows the harlequin figure to move differentially out of rank.

Kinetic Cube

It's always advisable to screw panels into position rather than glue them, irrevocably sealed. Then, if a malfunction should occur, the piece can be dismantled for repair. I always try to leave an 'escape hatch' for this purpose.

However, this particular box of tricks is sealed because of its construction. The five discs, driven at different speeds by two electric motors and gearing, cover all points of entry, except the base.

I forget its precise workings and am reminded of Robert Browning, who, when asked to explain his poetry, answered that when he wrote it, only God and Robert Browning knew what it meant. 'Now', said the poet, 'Only God knows!'

Noah's Ark Peepshow

A drum showing my illustrations for a Noah's Ark Frieze rotates within an outer drum containing a window. Through it, Noah and all the animals pass by, on a turntable powered by a size D, 1.5 volt battery. The Sundoves leitmotif which runs through my work, here, plays a celestial role.

Carousel

In Victorian times toy roundabouts were made with clockwork mechanisms, sometimes incorporating musical movements. My model is silent and driven by a clock movement powered by a size D, 1.5 volt battery.

The balance wheel was de-activated to produce a fast speed to turn the flag, a medium speed to control the column and horses and a slow speed to rotate the base. Thus, each collet for second-hand, minute-hand and hour-hand is utilized to move different parts of the carousel.

The photograph below shows how the drum is constructed in stages. Plywood strips are glued between the top and bottom discs. Plastic wood is applied, then sanded, painted and varnished.

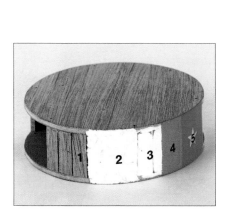

The Americanization of Georgia (opposite)

Georgia, my eldest granddaughter, was born in Los Angeles. I made this piece to celebrate her British roots while paying tribute to the American way of life she now enjoys.

Two motors run this very large automaton: a 6rpm rotary motor and a stapling machine with a DC motor linked to a 12 volt car battery charger, giving a powerful rocking movement. The activity is as follows:

Georgia rocks to and fro, clutching her Union Jack

Superman swoops from side to side on a wire, over a fractured *Hollywood Sign* and *Monument Valley*

A Coca-Cola bottle rocks behind *The Statue of Liberty* whose torch flame bobs up and down as radiating points spin above her head

The Mount Rushmore Presidents overlook *Mickey Mouse* jigging up and down and *Abe Lincoln* slowly revolves clipping *Johnny Reb's* head at every turn

Uncle Sam rocks back and forth, holding *'Old Glory'* and bowing to the baby (doll), Georgia

Charlie Brown, clutching a *baseball,* wobbles on a spring reeling from successive strikes of of a *baseball bat*

Charlie Chaplin, ostracized, hops up and down on his exiled platform

And lastly, the *Liberty Bell* rings at every beat of the humming machine

Space Frames

In November 1982 the Tate Gallery in London staged a wonderfully inspiring exhibition by the Swiss artist Jean Tinguely. The large and small space frames are an acknowledgement of his influence. He himself was an admirer of Calder and Duchamp finding precedents in their work for his own kinetic experiments.

My small space frame is powered by a 6rpm motor, while the larger version, originally made to take a 25rpm motor, I converted to hand cranked operation for exhibitions.

Bicycle Clock (Electric)

All my cyclists have a 'buck-up' cam on the inside buttock which, when contacting the lower torso, throws the figure forward, allowing it to fall back until the next contact. A certain urgency in cycling style is thus achieved.

Since the torque of an electric clock second hand cannot be overtaxed, my stovepipe-hatted gent is made from thin plasticard. A counter-weight is added at the rear to eliminate 'wheelies'!

Rainbow Clock (Clockwork) (opposite)

A 'Westminster Chimes' striking movement, with wires attached to the hammers, animates this clock. A flexible band and pulley, with the aid of a bevel gear, does the rest.

As the quarters are struck, the four doves, one attached to each hammer, rise and fall at each chime. Concurrently, the doves within the cloud-shaped aperture rotate laterally on a bevel gear, the shaft of which turns the sun in the foreground.

This performance is repeated on the hour with the added movement of the transparent sun, attached to the striking mechanism, from east to west; a notch at a time, and all the way over for 12 o'clock.

'Bluebelles' Clock (Electric)

These dancing girls perform as all troupers should: in step. All, that is, except for the blonde in the middle. She alone stares straight ahead, oblivious of the critical glances of the other dancers.

While the clock performs its usual function a secondary 8rpm motor turns the cams to animate the dancers. On the hour, a timer ensures, the high-stepping troupe come in on cue. And, of course, the blonde is out of step.

I made a larger version of *The Bluebelles* which was sold at an automata exhibition in Munich. The size allowed me to use more sophisticated animation, with mobile-breasted dancers who turned their heads as they kicked.

The original troupe can be seen as 'Nine Ladies Dancing' in my *Twelve Days of Christmas* automata on pages 28-29.

Uncle Sam's Clock (Electric)
Based on my Uncle Sam Whirligigs (pages 32-33), this is my favourite clock. The mesmerising slowness of the figures bowing to each other is amusing. Brass tubing provides the crank handle which fits on to the second-hand collet.

Black Owl Clock (Electric)
Two electric clock motors, stripped down to rotating discs, animate the 'wobbly' eyes.

An electric clock motor tells the time while the beak rotates on the second hand.

Star Wheel Clock (Electric)
Two motors operate this clock. One tells the time and turns the red, second-hand, star wheel. The other, in the base, drives the blue cog wheel which engages the yellow wheel to time a four-minute egg!

'Leotard' Clock (Electric)
Unlike the erratically versatile *Sand-Toy Leotard* (page 13), this trapeze *artiste* flips over the bar with predictable regularity, following his clockwise course. Not for him the thrills and disappointments of his sand-toy kinsman.

Sundoves Alarm Clock (Battery) (opposite)
It's fairly unusual to find modern quartz clocks which have synchronous movements. The Braun alarm clock, powered by a size C, 1.5 volt battery, is an exception, however. It gives a smooth rotary movement to the second-hand, rather than the jerky jumps associated with most quartz clocks.

With acknowledgements to Mr Braun, I have endeavoured to enhance his excellent alarm function by building a zig-zag section into the case. If this doesn't actually improve the sound quality, it looks as if it should!

Sundoves Clock (Electric)
'Sundoves' is a theme which, as I've mentioned on page 64, *Noah's Ark Peepshow*, runs through my work. The idea came to me watching television pictures of the sun in close-up. Flames licking the sun's perimeter looked like birds, of equal size, flapping their wings in a rotary motion. It was, I thought, an ideal image for a clock.

The decorative metallic foil I used radiates attractively in motion. The doves wheel is fixed to the second-hand and the hour-hand carries an orange sun. Since the foil is the same both sides and self-adhesive, the face is stuck to the glass. This allows the doves to rotate behind it and in front of the sun.

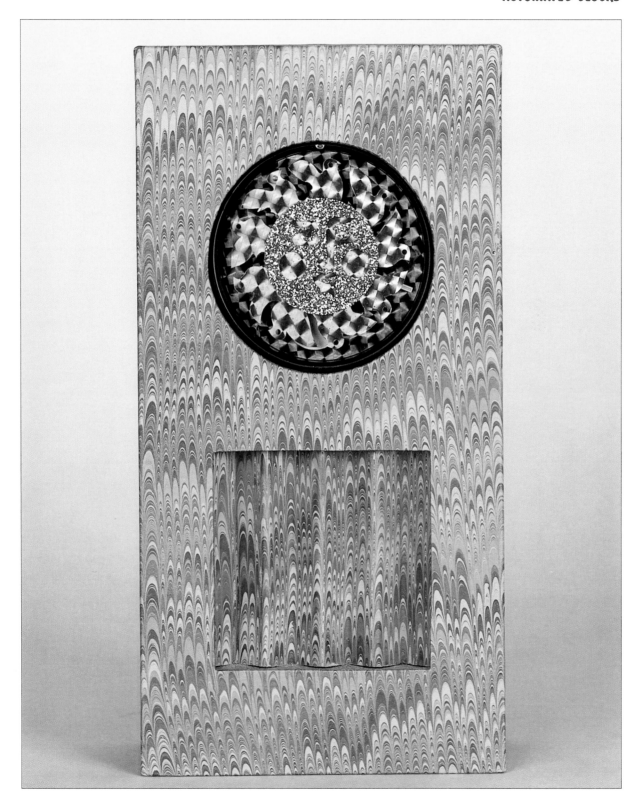

Tell the Time with Mortimer (Clockwork Alarm)
I made this alarm clock originally for a children's Breakfast TV programme. However, it was never used and I salvaged it to serve as a model from which to draw one of my picture books.

The Chinese movement includes an all-important date mechanism which is utilised for the blink. The alarm mechanism itself works the arms which furiously, alternately, hammer the bell. The clock hands whizz around and so, for good measure, does the nose! That's on the second-hand collet. Of course, the balance wheel was cut out to allow for all this animation.

Huxley Pig's Plane Clock (Electric)
Sometimes an electric clock second-hand is set *behind* the hour and minute-hands. This is fortuitous when a large image such as Huxley's plane is required to move *under* the clock hands.

Hollywood Clock (Electric)

This was a wedding present I made for my elder son and daughter-in-law. He is a writer and editor and she is also a writer in Hollywood. Making no concession to their generation of screen idols, I paid my tribute to the earlier, more glamourous Hollywood of my childhood.

I wanted an *Art Deco* look and built my idea for the clock on two plastic caryatids I salvaged from packaging on a Greek brandy bottle. (An idea can often start that way.)

The canopy housing the Hollywood sign is reminiscent of the Hollywood Bowl, open to the starry Los Angeles night sky. And the somewhat childish calligraphy derives from the cement writings of the stars, outside the famous Chinese Theatre.

Mechanically, this is another example of a second-hand being set *under* the hour and minute-hands. It allows a large cam to rotate, behind the façade, engaging ball-headed pins which ride on the cam's edge, or rim. These pins support the weighted letters which move up and down.

Through the window on the clock face we see screen legends pass by: Clark Gable and Vivien Leigh, Judy Garland, Cary Grant, John Wayne, Gary Cooper and Marilyn Monroe.

Looking at this glittering clock I am reminded of Oscar Levant's famous remark: 'Strip the phoney tinsel off Hollywood and you'll find the real tinsel underneath.'

'La Lola' Clock (Electric) 'La Lola' is derived, in name only, from that wonderful picture by Degas in London's Tate Gallery. It shows a circus performer hanging by her teeth from a rope. My *artiste* is suspended by a cord, turned by a clock mechanism concealed in the canopy. The leads run down one of the poles, made of brass tubing, and join the clock's leads in the base.

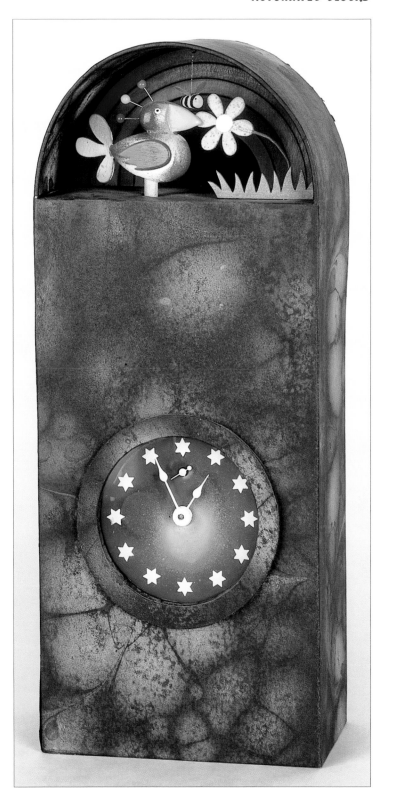

Flowerbird Musical Clock
(Clockwork)
The thirty-hour movement is connected at the a base to a metal drum with little teeth which engage a metal comb, in the manner of old musical boxes, when the alarm is released.

The pulley, connected to the alarm mechanism, operates a bevel gear under the bird which sets off the animation. As the bird rotates to the music, its beak knocks the flower (the stalk being a flexible spring) which, in turn, nudges the bee suspended by invisible nylon thread.

These boxes are both useful and decorative. They look equally at home in the kitchen or on bookshelves and even mounted on brackets. They are ideal for storing those little things which struggle for attention in drawers, like stock cubes or string, pens and pencils and postcards. In fact, anything that would like to live in a miniature home.

Some of my boxes have a retaining bar at the base to prevent things from falling out. A magnet is embedded in the bar which, when in contact with another magnet, or piece of metal stuck to the reverse of the façade, creates a magnetic latch.

Park House (opposite)
So called because my wife and I lived in Park House, Cheltenham. The façade is hinged on the left with a retaining bar and magnetic latch.

Peach House (above)
The roof lifts off, as a lid.

Pink House (left)
The roof is hinged on the left for opening.

Grey House (opposite)
The façade is hinged on the left with a retaining bar inside, housing a magnetic latch.

Green House
The façade is hinged on the left, with a magnetic latch. It has a central shelf and serves as a spice box.

Noah's Ark (opposite)
The ultimate house box contains Mr and Mrs Noah and the animals, all neatly arranged in a box. The puzzle element is enhanced by a surprise build-it-yourself rainbow concealed under the deck.

Quilt House
Made for my wife, Tatjana, a quilter. The roof is hinged at the back.

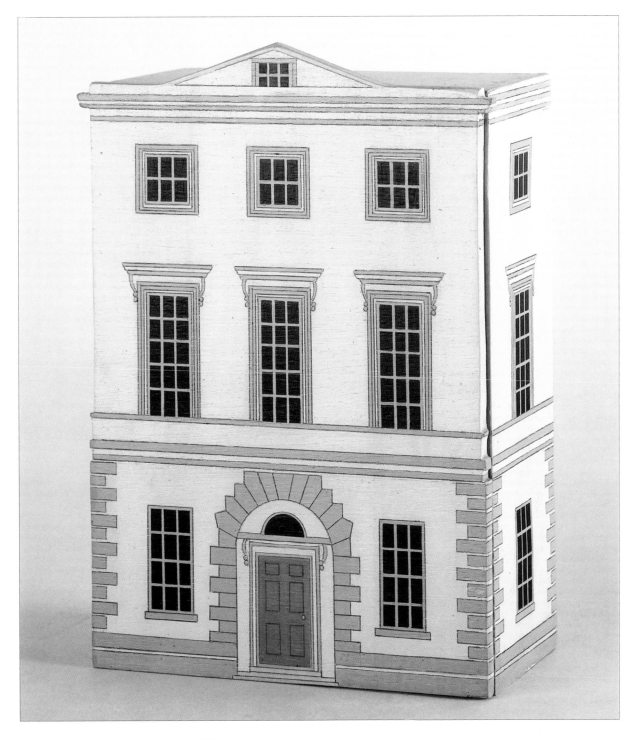

Town Houses I and II
These were designed, as a pair, to go on brackets. *Town House I* is c.1775 and
Town House II is c.1745.

TOY WITH THE IDEA

The getting of an idea is one thing, making it work is quite another. Like a cornerstone, sometimes an idea needs to support a whole structure. We need to be able to lay bricks, render and paint them, safe in the knowledge that our structure is sound. Sound enough to add storeys if we want. We can call this a 'structural idea', as its basis is in a solid, sensible framework.

In my talks to children during my *Toy with the Idea* touring exhibitions, I used another analogy, to explain how I got my ideas. They were, I suggested, little sparks which could light a fire. Each flame could make another flame until you had a blazing bonfire of sparkling ideas! We can call this a 'mercurial idea'. Its basis is in ingenuity and inspiration.

For my picture book *The Mice who Lived in a Shoe* the spark that lit my bonfire was a pair of 'Hush Puppy' shoes. I was, at the time, considering doing a picture book based on the well-known nursery rhyme *The Old Woman Who Lived in a Shoe*. The shoes, I thought, would be ideal for making two models: one showing the framework, and the other the completed shoe-house. I would use them for reference to draw my illustrations.

Many illustrators use pictorial reference, but if none exists one solution is to make it oneself. Since I had just had my book published on *Moving Toys,* modelmaking my own reference seemed a good solution. As I began to work on my model it nagged at me that perhaps I was not getting the most out of the idea. After all, I was merely illustrating a well-known rhyme, something I had done several times before. It occurred to me that with a slight change of direction the notion could be improved. Unwittingly I had provided the catalyst in my initial drawings.

Among my first sketches of the old woman, her children and the shoe-house I had drawn an unrelated doodle of a little mouse, in costume. Doodles, as we all know, can be the parents of successful ideas. They are manifestations of the neutral mind, which can be most productive. And so it proved to be.

I evicted the Old Woman and her charges and installed a family of mice. They were, after all, shoe-sized! I jettisoned the rhyme too, of course, and set about writing the story where the family of mice built, from a leaky old shoe, a wonderful shoe-house to shelter from the weather and the unwanted attentions of the neighbourhood cat. (page 100)

The 'structural idea' literally, in this case, of making a model shoe-house and the 'mercurial idea' of switching to mice, were fused into one creative platform. It enabled me to operate as a modelmaker, author and illustrator of what eventually became a series of six picturebooks. Significantly, it allowed me, having set my own limits, to erect a signpost for sequels to follow.

I made many models for the *Mice* picturebooks, working with mice-sized household objects. A tea-kettle became a pirate ship in *The Kettleship Pirates*. A little sardine tin boat, with a leaf for a sail, accompanied it. There followed, over some years, an aeroplane constructed from miniature baskets, a clockwork bus made from an alarm clock and a sola topi, a lunar module egg box and a bowler hat which flew in the air, ran on the road, and sailed on water.

It's lovely when ideas, especially ideas with mileage, work for us. But sometimes we produce sparks and the bonfire just won't light. Poke around as we may, the flames are uncoordinated, won't link up and ignite. And then suddenly a burst of flame and the bonfire blazes! The unexpected surprises and rewards us.

It is almost as if a passing angel pops the idea into our heads. Angels are a current theme of mine since I created *Angelmouse* for BBC Television. His genesis was not in a burst of flame but in a series of sparks which only ignited once I had thought of his companion. I wanted to do a story about a little toy mouse, but I needed him to be different in some special way from other mice in children's stories; not least my own *The Mice Who Lived in a Shoe*.

I wanted my mouse to have a close friend of about the same size and decided upon a bird. As the bird had wings then so could the mouse, I reasoned. A flying mouse? They could now be together throughout the story. It was then only a short step to make the connection: a mouse angel: *Angelmouse*.

A precursor to *Angelmouse* was *Huxley Pig*. He arrived in the lazy, easy, way. A burst of flame, a flash, whatever it is that happens when an idea comes out of the blue. I awoke one December morning on the dot of six o'clock with the name Huxley Pig on my lips. I asked my wife what she thought of that as a name for a character.

I got my seal of approval and started at once to make a little articulated wooden pig. My mother, an expert doll maker, made costumes for Huxley to my designs. Her wonderful interpretations served not only to supply excellent reference for me but also for the animation company who made the *Huxley Pig* series for television. (page 112)

The pig needed props, so I made a bed for which my wife stitched a little quilt. Also he required a suitcase to keep his costumes in. He would be a daydreaming pig, I decided, and would dress up for each daydreaming adventure. (page 115)

It's interesting, the sudden way Huxley came to me; almost pre-packaged, just as I awoke. These early moments, like those late at night, seem to be good times to get ideas. The mind is rested, either waking from, or dropping into, an almost dreaming state. Drowsiness is next to Godliness, perhaps!

As a foil to writing the *Huxley Pig* scripts I wanted to undertake something totally unrelated to them. For some time I had toyed with the idea of making THE TWELVE DAYS OF CHRISTMAS (pages 28-29) as several automata in one whole piece. It would have to work both mechanically and aesthetically – a perfect example, in fact, of the 'structural' and 'mercurial' ideas fusing into one.

Once I'd made the automata I was encouraged to look for other subjects in the public domain, a rich source of ideas, which come as a gift.

We all have our favourite themes and invest them with our own particular passions. Some of mine include Blake's TYGER! TYGER! (pages 36-37) and American influences like UNCLE SAM (pages 32-33, 60 and 73) or the HOLLYWOOD SIGN (pages 38-39). But if there is one of my automata which expresses most clearly the aims and directions of this book, it is A DIFFERENT DRUMMER (pages 62-63). Let Thoreau have his say:

> If a man does not keep pace with
> his companions, perhaps it is because
> he hears a different drummer.
> Let him step to the music he hears,
> however measured or far away.

Toy with the idea. Think about it. Make it.

TOY WITH THE IDEA

MICE MODELS

HUXLEY PIG MODELS

CHARACTER MODELS

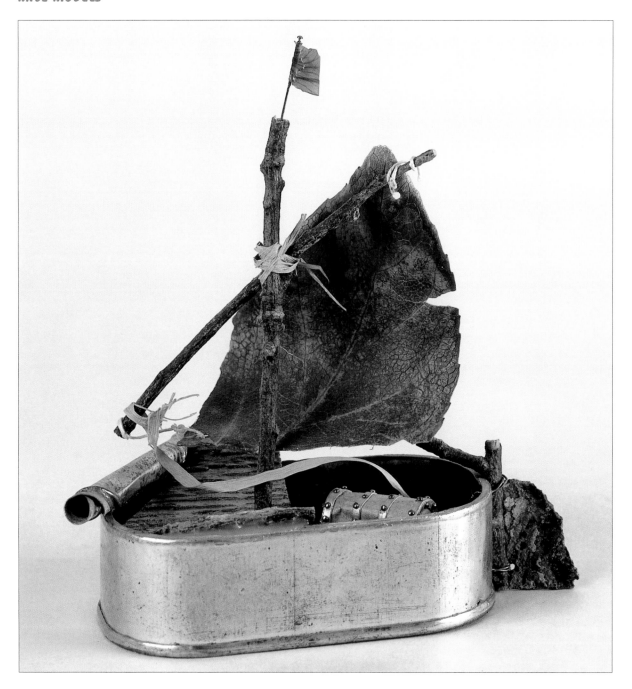

Sardine Tin Boat
This was the subsidiary model for *The Kettleship Pirates*, the first sequel to *The Mice Who Lived in a Shoe*. The deck and rudder were made from bark, while a twig and leaf provided me with a mast and sail. The treasure chest was made from card, filled with PVA white glue and pierced with pins to look like studs. When the glue contracted, on drying, the chest assumed a suitably battered effect.

In 1981 my picture book *The Mice who Lived in a Shoe* was published in England by Penguin Books under the Viking Kestrel imprint and in America by Lothrop Lee and Shepard. Various European publishers took it, together with Japan and China.

There followed, over a decade, five sequels of my mice Family. For each book I made two models: a main model and a subsidiary model. Around them I hatched the stories and wrote the texts. I then used the models as reference for my illustrations.

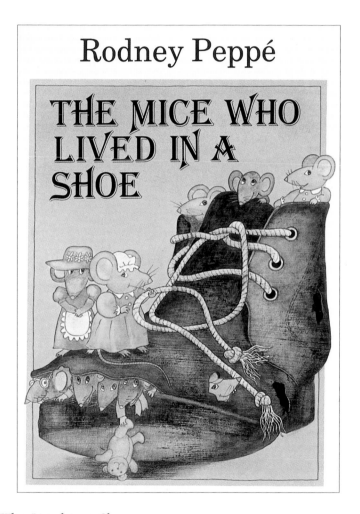

The Mice Who Lived in a Shoe
This is a story of a large family of mice who live in an old shoe which leaks when it rains and wobbles when the wind blows. So the mice decide to rebuild their home...

Skeleton Shoe House
As the story structure grew, so did the model making. The right shoe housed my main model and now I used the left shoe to show the framework.

Shoe House (opposite)
The shoe was first filled with plaster to give it stability, and the structure set into it. Delicate features such as the play platform and balconies could then be added to the solid shoe without fear of movement.

The ship and its crew sailed through fog.

They sailed into storms.

The Kettleship Pirates

This, the second book in the series, was published in 1983. Pip the mouse spies a pirate's hat and, nearby, a pirate ship fashioned from an old kettle and filled with, what else, Kettleship Pirates.

Kettleship (opposite)

The trickiest part was drilling holes through the kettle handle to hold the three masts. The cannons were made from dowel with thick soldering wire round the barrels. Silver paint and instant glue did the rest.

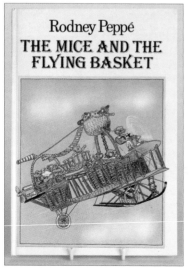

Flying Dart
This evil-looking machine belongs to Baron von Rathoven, the villain in *The Mice and the Flying Basket*. The seat is made of Milliput, a versatile putty, which becomes rock-hard when set.

The Mice and the Flying Basket
The third book in the series was published in 1985. The mice are in trouble. They work hard at making baskets for D. Rat, the junk merchant, but they never earn enough money to feed themselves. So they decide to build a flying basket and win first prize at the Air Show!

Flying Basket
This utilizes miniature baskets, made in Taiwan. After that I was on my own!
There are three electric motors. The power for the helicopter motor goes up
the rope ladder from a size D, 1.5 volt battery below the main deck, which also
feeds the forward propeller and lights. The rear motor has its own size C, 1.5
volt battery under the hatch.

Rollerskate Bus
Known in *The Mice and the Clockwork Bus* as D. Rat's rattletrap, this bicycle bus is the cause of the mice's discontent. It is made from a child's rollerskate, leather, laces and a cotton reel.

Clockwork Bus (opposite)
The idea for this was conceived when my wife was given a brand new pith helmet, or sola topi. Since we had no immediate plans to go to India it became the basis for this book. The chassis is an old door lock and the motor an old alarm clock.

The Mice and the Clockwork Bus
This was published in 1985. D. Rat's bicycle bus is so dangerous and overcrowded that everyone calls it the Rattletrap. But it's the only bus service for miles so the resourceful mice family do the only possible thing – they build their own bus.

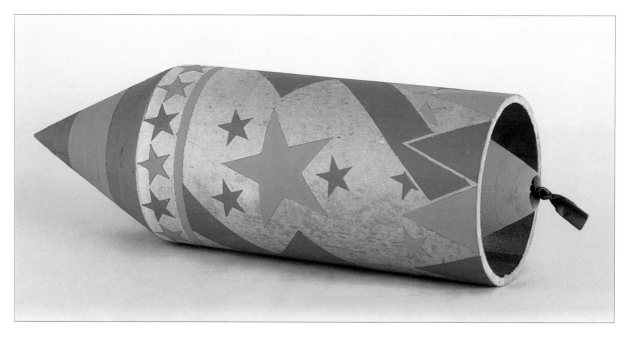

Moonrocket Firework
Made from a large cardboard roll, this rocket transports the mice, after separation, halfway to the moon. The rest of the journey is completed by D. Rat, a stowaway aboard the rocket.

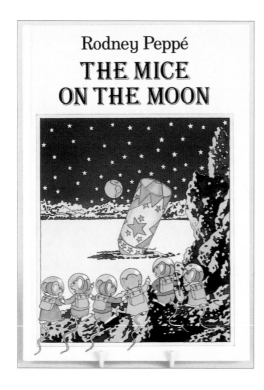

The Mice on the Moon (left)
The penultimate book in the series was published in 1992. The mice decide to build a spaceship and fly to the moon. But will wicked D. Rat, the junk merchant, try to interfere with their plans?

Lunar Module Egg Box (opposite)
The simplest main model in the series for *The Mice on the Moon* was built around an egg carton for the body of the space ship. I fitted washers for portholes, plastic straws for the legs and large screw-head covers for the feet. Blue celluloid and miniature hinges provided the solar panel.

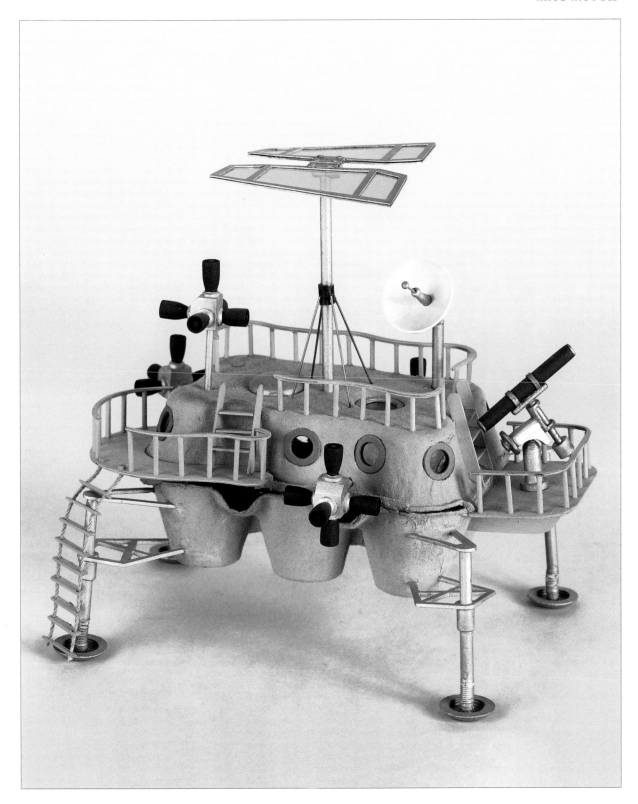

Travelling Toilet Roll
This elegant machine, together with its pilot, D. Rat, comes to a sticky end over the Arizona desert in *The Mice and the Travel Machine*.

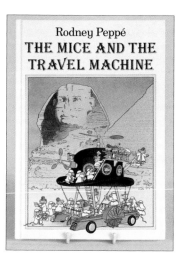

The Mice and the Travel Machine
In 1993 the final *Mice* book was published. The mice who live in a shoe find an old bowler hat in D. Rat's junkyard. They want a holiday but can't afford the travel fares and so they decide to build an ingenious travel machine. But of course D. Rat is on hand to thwart their round-the-world plans.

Travel Machine
My father's old bowler hat provided me with the last model in the series. I had to build something which would fly in the air, run on the road and sail in the water. The result was a helicopter-lorry-catamaran.

The genesis of Huxley Pig is covered on page 96. Although invented in a flash, I had to harness that invention in tangible form. First I made sketches of the pig, having no idea what story-lines I would employ. Although he had a name, he did not, as yet, possess a character. That would come much later. But I knew roughly what sort of pig I wanted to make and hoped the stories would flow from that.

Eventually they did and Huxley developed from a book character into a television character. A supporting cast was invented and two series of thirteen ten-minute episodes were filmed for Central Television. Martin Jarvis voiced the characters and I wrote the scripts for the production company, FilmFair.

The Original Huxley Pig (left and opposite)
I cut profiled sections in wood of the head
and body, then glued and clamped them in
a vice. Individual limbs were designed, cut
and jointed. Then everything was moulded
into shape using rasps, files, flap-wheels
and finally fine sandpaper. I assembled a
nude articulated pig. Even his ears moved.
But it was not a pretty sight!

The pig needed clothes, so he was
despatched to my mother, an expert with
the needle. Working from my drawings she
produced six wonderful outfits creating,
with skill and imagination, much more than
I had indicated in my original sketches.

Huxley was now in a state to be drawn in
any of his costumes for the picture books.
Eventually the costumes provided reference
for the film puppet Huxley, the daydreaming pig.

Photographs: Frederick Warne/The Penguin Group

Photographs: Frederick Warne/The Penguin Group

Huxley Pig's Props

Huxley's bed, boat and suitcase were items I made originally for my own reference in drawing the picture books. However, it wasn't long before they served as models for the film production company to work from.

The quilt and the bedding were made by my wife who is a textile artist; the boat was magnified as an exact replica to hold Huxley and his crew; and the suitcase was copied closely, using my photographically reduced travel labels stuck on to brown boot polished cardboard, simulating leather.

Huxley Pig's Motor Car
This was a model I built to come apart. The story I wrote told of a motor car kit given to Huxley. He day-dreams himself into a full-sized car with all the travelling consequences.

Huxley Pig's Aeroplane
The Aeroplane was made from seven layers of MDF which were glued and clamped together. These were then shaped by sanding and filling to provide a smooth surface for painting. Adhesive masks were cut for painting the crisp lines and shapes.

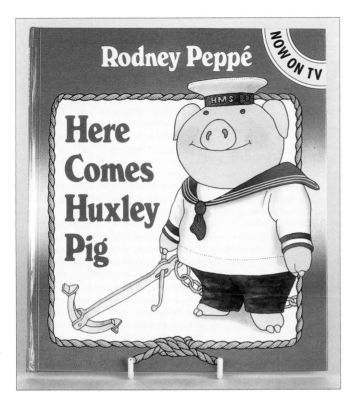

Huxley Pig Picture Books
These show the illustrations based on the models I made for my own reference.

Huxley Pig Pebbles (opposite)
Each Christmas, for four years, I painted a wooden pebble for my wife. I started with the sailor Huxley in 1987. The clown, winter-woolly and town clothes followed.

Henry the Elephant

Henry was my first venture into making articulated 3-D characters as lay figures for my picture book illustrations. I got the idea from a book about the Disney studios, which showed puppets made to guide the animators.

Armed with this (for me) exciting approach to drawing I wanted to make a character for my next picture book. I had done an Alphabet and Counting book, and Nursery Rhyme books, but never one about a character. As I've always had a fondness for elephants – paradoxically, ever since I fell off one in India as a child – I chose a little elephant, Henry, for my debut into original storytelling.

I carved Henry from solid wood; not in sections, as I did for later models. The block dictated my carving and I soon eschewed my original drawings for the model in my head. However, the empirical nature of my whittling produced too long a body and I had to saw out a section from the middle.

Since Henry turned at the waist on a dowel rod, the loss of midriff necessitated two cuts instead of one. His body, limbs and trunk are all held together with elastic and his ears are hinged with leather supported by blu-tak.

Huxley Pig and Horace
Huxley and his aeroplane have already made an appearance in these pages (page 117). Now the rotten rodent Horace joins Huxley. He is his nemesis in the books and the television programmes. It is only by his wheedling ways that Horace has made it into this book!

   Horace's genesis is very doubtful indeed. Under all that fur and gum arabic is a vandalized teddy bear. A modelling compound, Das, was used to model his form over the unfortunate teddy.

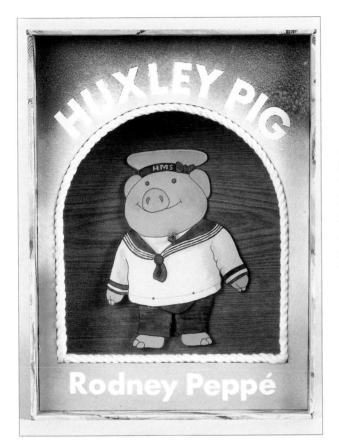

Huxley Pig Display Model I (Battery)
Somewhat faded by exposure in bookshop windows and exhibitions, the dancing sailor Huxley uses the magnetic mechanics of an old advertising display unit. Powered by a size D, 1.5 volt battery, he dances a very realistic hornpipe on a rocker concealed within.

Huxley Pig Display Model II (Electric)
Here, in his winter woolly outfit, Huxley performs like a jumping jack, but slowly. An 8rpm motor turns a disc inside, with a dowel which pulls on the string to activate his limbs.

Gus, the Cat

Originally carved in wood, like the rest of the model, Gus's head underwent changes. These were made at the request of my publisher, HarperCollins, who published my picture book *Gus and Nipper* in 1996. I added a modelling compound, Das, to make the necessary amendments, which were not apparent once I repainted the head. My wife, Tatjana, clothed the model and I used it as a lay figure from which to draw.

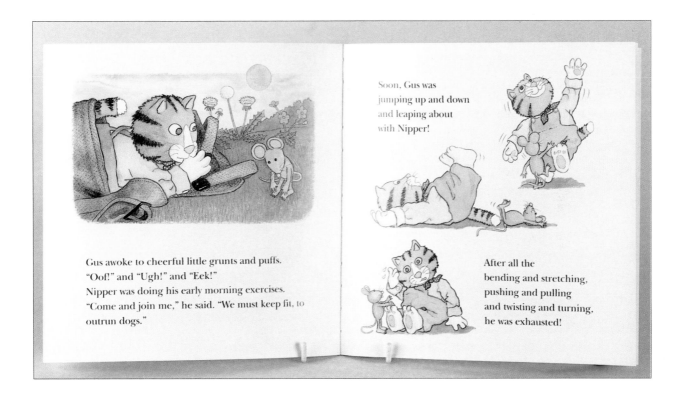

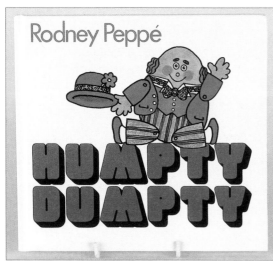

Humpty Dumpty Cut-Out
My first excursion into making a flat lay figure
from which to draw my illustrations was
Humpty Dumpty (Viking Kestrel, 1974). At the
end of the book young readers were invited
to put Humpty together again, using simple
instructions. A pebble Humpty is typical of the
artefacts I make from my books.

Pip Mouse of the MICE Books
This is the only instance where I made a model based on one of my drawings,
rather than the other way round. I was invited to make the model of Pip, the
hero of *The Mice Who Lived in a Shoe*, and its sequels, by a TV animation
production company. Its purpose was to spearhead a presentation for puppet
animation, but the project stalled.

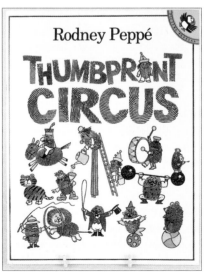

Thumbprint Circus
Book proofs can come in useful, especially if one asks for two sets of proofs: one to keep and one to mark up and send back to the publishers.

I pasted the page proofs of my picture book *Thumbprint Circus* (Viking Kestrel, 1988) on to skin-ply, cut them out and made the circus scene. It is housed under a dome as it's difficult to dust!

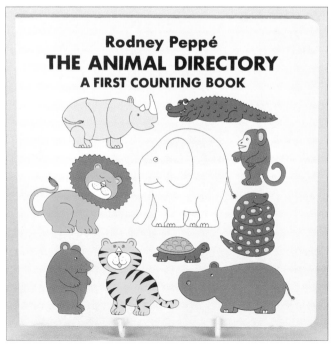

Cardboard Zoo
For my counting book, *The Animal Directory* (Blackie, 1989), I cut out plasticard templates from which to draw the animals. They came in handy to make the corrugated cardboard zoo.

The animals were cut out on a scroll saw, four at a time which, by the nature of the material, provided little resistance to the saw blade. String and a little drawing and painting completed the project.

CONCLUSION

All the toys, models and automata within these pages owe their existence, in some measure, to the gifts of concentration and patience passed down to me from my mother's side of the family. Any manipulative skills and even talent would be somewhat strained without these advantages.

The less inspiring aspects of working in wood, be it shaping, sanding and indeed any preparatory work, need those qualities of concentration and patience as bulwarks against the temptation of reaching a finished state too soon. Time should play a subsidiary role in the equation to excellence – excellence in both concept and execution. It takes as long as it takes to produce high quality work and to cut corners to meet deadlines or fulfil financial strictures is really the province of the factory; not the individual maker. If you do have a deadline, allow for contingencies.

I am reminded of the hours my late mother spent on her passion for an 1872 dolls' house which she refurbished, inside and out, over a period of twenty years. She made most of the furniture and as an expert doll maker created a doll family with resident cook and visiting friend. I made, amongst other items, a couple of lacquered clocks for her: An Act of Parliament (or Tavern) clock for the kitchen and a longcase clock for the hall (see over page).

In time, the dolls' house came to me and eventually I passed it on to my son Jonathan, a painter and sculptor who makes very individual dolls' houses. He too is the beneficiary of genes conveying concentration and patience. These qualities should not be overestimated, however; they are merely advantages. They weigh little against, say, the quality of passion which brings vibrance to the work and ultimately reveals talent.

Talent is rather like an iceberg: we generally see only the tip. For some reason most of us seem incapable of using all that we have been given (just as we are told that we only use a portion of our brains). It depends on the size of the iceberg, of course. Da Vinci's or Picasso's iceberg would probably have sunk the *Titanic*. We, lesser mortals, must be content to know that talent can be developed from below the waterline, so to speak.

Laziness is probably our worst enemy. It deprives us of pushing creative endeavour to its limits, preferring to rest on the laurels of tried and tested solutions. It is really a question of going the extra mile: of asking ourselves whether we have achieved the most out of what we have created. Could it be improved, simplified perhaps?

Another demon to accompany laziness (in fact it probably causes it) is false contentment. We fool ourselves that we have done our best when, deep down, we know that the piece we have made is not quite up to scratch. We have to be our own severest critics here, even if it means starting again. Just put it down to experience and move forward.

Our creative legacies encompass various qualities and talents and it is up to us to use them to the fullest. In the Introduction I expressed a hope that readers might be inspired to take the plunge and make their own pieces. To those still standing on the diving board, I urge them to make the dive.

Come on in, the water's lovely!

Dolls' House Clocks
I made these for my mother's 1872 dolls' house at a scale of one inch to the foot. The Act of Parliament Clock, so named because of a tax imposed on clocks in 1797 and repealed the following year, is 5¾in (146mm) high. It hangs in the kitchen.

The longcase clock is 7in (178mm) tall and stands in the hall. Both clocks are made from 6-sheet mounting board and painted with acrylics and gold paint to simulate Chinese lacquer, which was popular in the mid-eighteenth century. The twisted pillars are made from soldering wire and painted gold.

PLANS

Although *Toy with the Idea* is not a 'how-to' book, I have included eight plans for making the simpler toys and models. Very basic instructions for these are below, with photographic references following the headings. The numerals denote the number of pieces to cut.

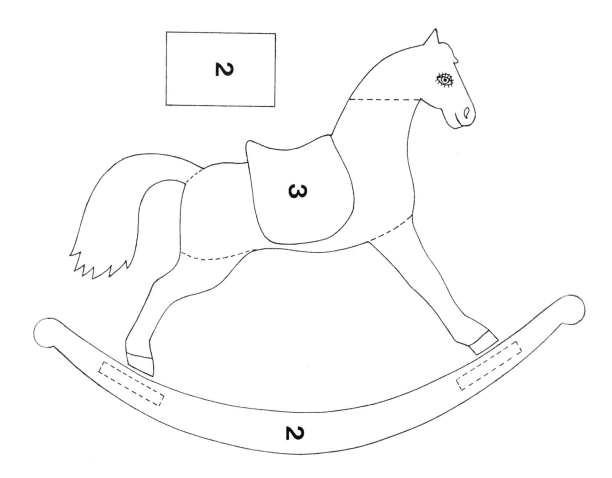

Rocking Horse (page 14)
Cut the three sections of the horse and the two rockers from 10mm (⅜in) softwood. The two rocker boards are cut from 4mm (⅛in) plywood and glued to the rockers. Shape the horse and decorate, using the picture as a guide.

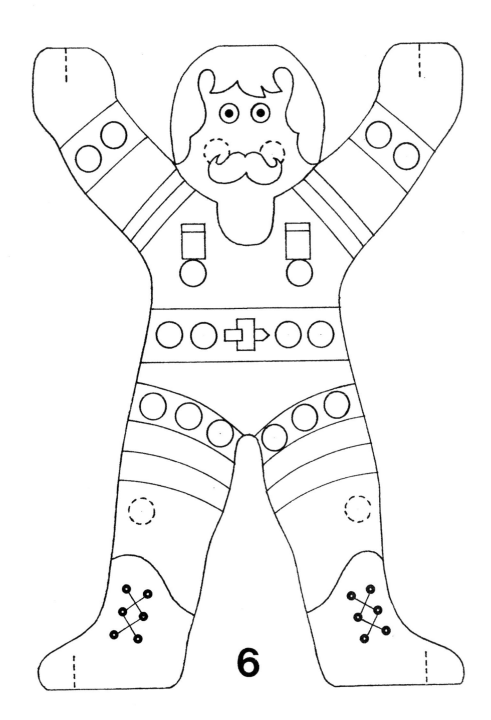

6

Hole-and-Peg Acrobats (pages 44-45)
Cut six figures from 12mm (½in) softwood. Drill 5mm (³⁄₁₆in) holes into the hands and feet as indicated on the plan.

Cut four 5mm (³⁄₁₆in) dowels 16mm (⅝n) long for each figure. Decorate, using the picture as a guide.

Bird Tree (page 46)
Cut out the tree and base support from 10mm (⅜in) softwood. Then cut out the birds as on the plan.

Bird and Worm Puzzle (page 46)
Cut from 10mm (⅜in) softwood.

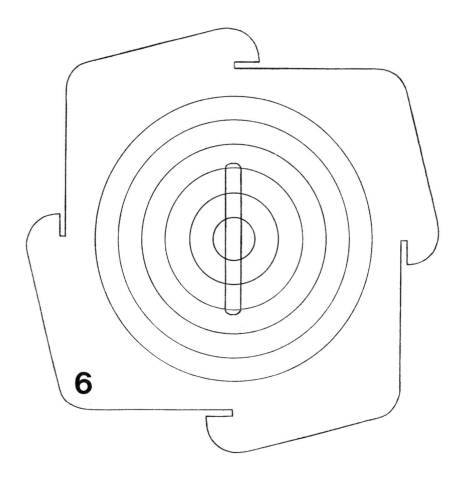

Money Box (page 47)
Cut from 1.5mm (¹⁄₁₆in) skin (Aero) ply. If you are drawing concentric circles, cut
the slot after painting.

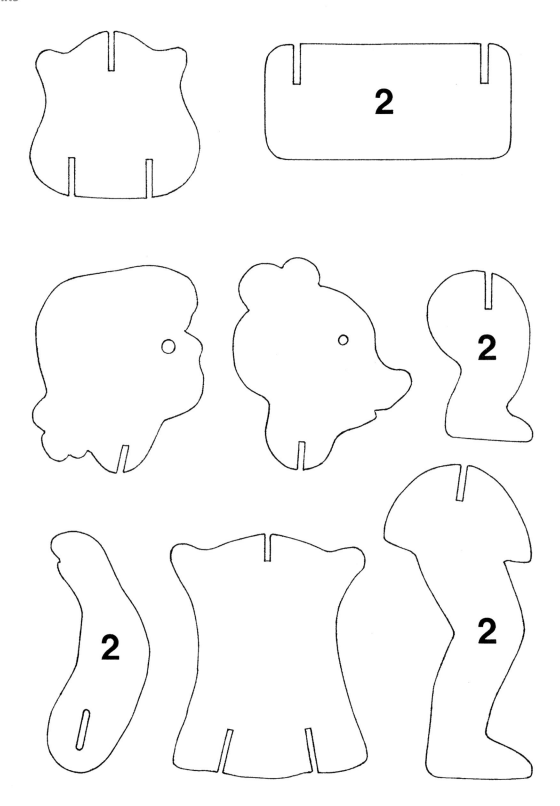

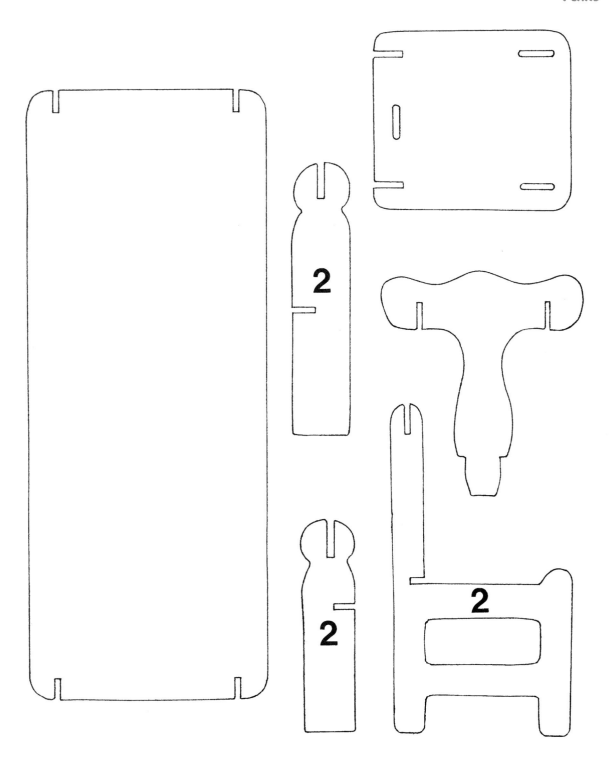

Goldilocks and the Three Bears (page 49)
Cut from 1.5mm (⅟₁₆in) skin (Aero) ply. Assemble as in the picture.

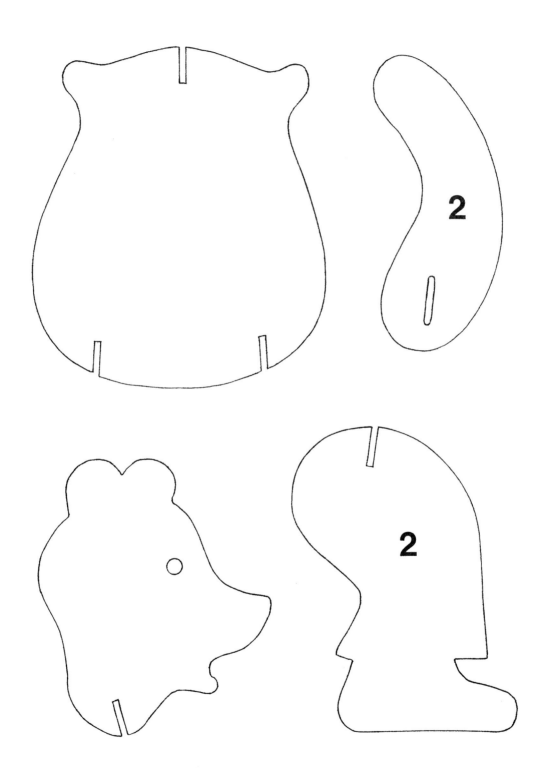

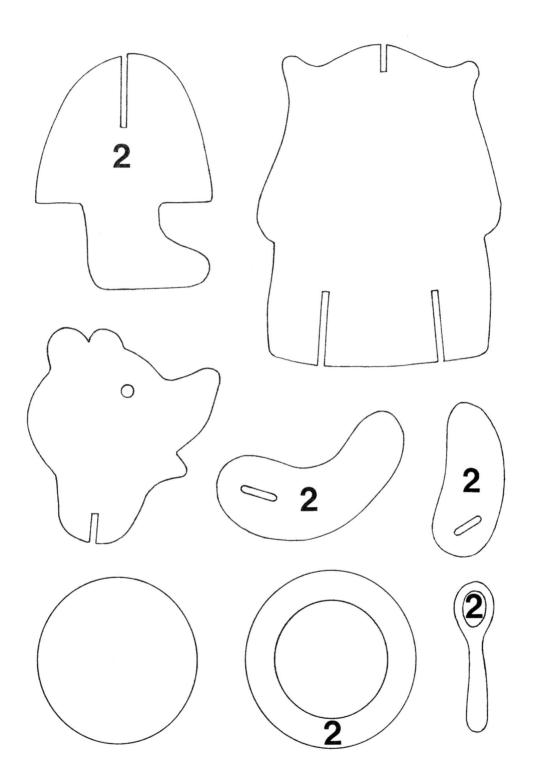

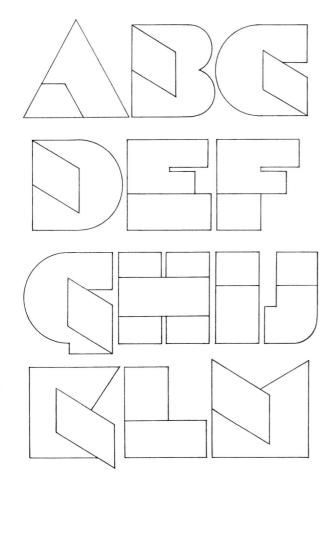

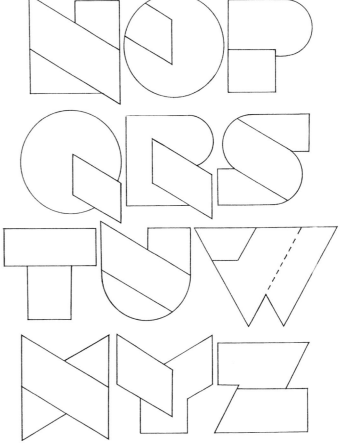

Cardboard Zoo (page 130)
Cut from 6mm (¼in) corrugated cardboard. Add string for the tails, and struts behind their legs for support.

Decorative Alphabet (page 49)
Cut from 10mm (⅜in) softwood.

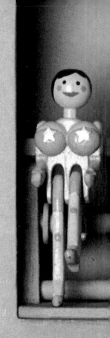

eight
maids a-milking

ten lords

eleven pip